Fifty Shades of Nagging
Most of Them Grey!

Chris Gibson

Published by alliebooks.co.uk

Fifty Shades of Nagging -
Most of Them Grey!
By Chris Gibson

Published by: alliebooks.co.uk
A Division of Franology Limited
158 Hermon Hill
South Woodford
London E18 1QH

ISBNs:
Parent: 978-1-909429-00-0
ePub version: 978-1-909429-02-4
Mobi version: 978-1-909429-01-7

Second Impression 2013 · Third Impresssion 2013
orders@alliebooks.co.uk
www.alliebooks.co.uk

ePublished by Original eBooks,
a division of Original Writing (UK) Limited· an Original Writing Group
company

British Library Cataloguing in Publication Data
A catalogue record for this book is available from the
British Library

This book is intended as a light·hearted observation of relationships only, not as a definitive
scientific manual. The opinions of the author are intended as a monologue and are in no way
intended to offend anyone. Any reference to an experience is not directed at any one individual
and any reference to an individual by name, implied in the narrative or any association is
purely coincidental. The author does not accept any liability in the event that any individual
assumes that any reference may be based on that individual.
Should any individual consider any of the narrative is directed at them then the author would
like to suggest that they shouldn't flatter themselves!

Contents

Preface

As he entered the room he immediately recognised the back of her hourglass figure, and as he admired the vision she ran her hand through her blonde locks carefully sweeping the fringe across and behind her left ear. For an instant he remembered the first time she wore that summer dress, and a wry smile replaced the vacant look as he recalled what happened that day, and all night.

As she turned their eyes met and he imagined diving into the pool that her blue eyes always reminded him of. Her lips were pressed together she moved towards him and before he could utter a word he found himself paralysed with anticipation, his heart pounding as if it was about to burst. She glanced to the floor, momentarily, before raising her piercing eyes slowly, taking in every inch of his tall frame before fixing her gaze on his slightly flushed face and after what seemed an eternity she parted her lips and said "Well hello, I've been waiting for you..."

The words were spoken in a soft and sultry tone, a tone that always made him feel warm inside. Just as he felt at ease she followed the pause with a silence, shaking her head slowly from side to side before taking a deep breath, her hands on her hips and with a look that Medusa would be proud of she said...

"So, come on where the bloody hell have you been, what have you been up to, you know this is my girls night out, I'm late now so we'll talk about this later?" Like an automatic weapon the shots kept coming and coming, penetrating in short bursts. The illusion was shattered, but he half expected it, after all they had been together for a few years now!

Sound Familiar? Just four of the cutting comments that are spoken and heard all over the world, every day! Thankfully this isn't written as a parody, it is more a collection of satirical examples for men and women to read and relate to.

Men stutter and flounder over a question, unsure of how to reply in case it they haven't understood the real meaning. Wouldn't it be great to respond with some alternative replies to show how crazy some of the questions or comments are? In this light-hearted look at words and statements that can chill you to the bone, make you feel guilty or leave you tongue-tied. We will take you on a man's journey through life, experiencing copious helpings of 'nag pie.'

Things aren't always black or white, there is a lot of grey and different shades of grey that all amount to one thing, nag pie! Of course this slice of pie might be deserved a lot of the time, but sometimes, just sometimes, men have absolutely no idea what they have done wrong.

About the Author

Chris Gibson in an author and co-author of many serious, well fairly serious, business books and spends the rest of his working life as a franchise consultant and a mentor-instructor for a global institution that provides education for individuals and corporate learners, a career that will probably be ruined by this tongue in cheek nonsense!

Aside for working for a living, he is a devoted father and spends as much time as he can enjoying life and avoiding 'nag pie', although he was lucky enough not to have too many portions in his married life!

Of course he acknowledges that 'nag pie' is most certainly deserved on occasion and in the past he has deserved a slice or two, but after nearly half a century of living amongst the female species he would prefer to avoid the 'game of slice' and speak openly.

This book is a culmination of years of first hand experience, of watching friends and families communicate, seeing outbursts in public places and hearing stories from friends that are in the doghouse!

Follow @ChrisGAuthor
Facebook - Chris Gibson Author Page

Acknowledgments

To my daughter Allie who has grown into a little woman far too quickly but has already shown signs of a becoming a fine baker of pies!

To my mother, who has not let up on judgment for the whole of my life... and to Don, my brother, for sharing the joys too.

In memory of Dad, thanks for the heads up in my formative years that all women are funny buggers, well actually the phrase was slightly more descriptive "all women are *******" can't even bring myself write it here!

To my estranged wife Helen, you should have been a crown prosecutor or a psychologist, but as a mother you are second to none.

To every other lady who has been close to me and has adorned the table with the finest slices of pie a man could wish for!

To Ian and Dac, from a conversation over a few beers one night, the inspiration to write this book, a genius conversation and a good night it was too!
(Wait for the third degree on that little comments boys!)

To the men and women of the world – nothing will change, bake, serve and consume.

Here's the serious bit. Sometimes 'nag pie' goes a little too far, both sides, and while this book is intended on the lighter-side it would be wrong not to acknowledge the existence of some who take it too far and make peoples lives miserable. If this book would show just one person that it's not worth it and save another from underserved grief then I will be a happy bunny. Laughter should be in everyone's daily routine; control and suppression is just wrong.

1
It's an age-old game!

Say what?

Do you always say the wrong thing or miss the real message from your partner?

If you do, guess what you are not alone. Ever since cavemen grunted at cavewomen they have had a grunt or two back which might have meant "how many times have I asked you to take the mammoth bones out" or "suppose you've been hunting with your mates again!"

Men and women have the ability to wind each other up not with just what they say to each other but how they say it. Here's the thing a woman can ask a question and she is really asking something different, men know this and they get flustered, answer in a way that makes them appear guilty and before they know it they face the Spanish Inquisition with a barrage of questions or comments. Instead of saying 'what are you really asking?' men get sucked into the game and then complain of nag pie!

In this light-hearted look at the things women say and what men translate the words into or what they would like to say back, it will become clear that in the 'communication pie chart' of any relationship some things are said on a regular basis and other ones come out of the blue; moreover there are many shades of 'nag pie', most of them grey. Men moan to their buddies about the comments and constant questions and call it 'nagging' or a slice of 'nag pie.' Whether you call it 'nag pie', discussion or a disagreement the fact remains that what one says to another is often different to what they are really saying. That's the funny side of life and the game that we all play.

Tongue in cheek it maybe, but the beauty is that even with the translations, or alternative sarcastic replies contained herein, the debate to the real meaning will continue, forever!

I can see it now; certain people in my life will probably think that this book is about them. Sorry to disappoint, but this creation is born out of nearly 50 years of living amongst the opposite sex. Some of it is personal, true, while some of it is gleaned from observation, people watching in truth. Ahh, people watching, one of the finest pastimes available to man and woman alike, seeing someone else give and receive a slice of 'nag pie'!

Wait a minute here I go doing what men do, explaining themselves in the hope that the 'reasoning' will protect them from an earful, tunnelling their way out of something they have said or done trying to make it all right again, after all if it makes sense to me so why the heck doesn't it make sense to you?

When faced with a question from our other halves, isn't it often an interrogation, an enigma wrapped up in mystery? We plead innocence and usually dig a deeper hole, it's a downward spiral and even if you are not guilty by the end of the exchange something else, something completely un-associated, will enter the argument; time to give up and face the sentencing! GUILTY!

How true is this? Who knows, it's an opinion, but one shared by millions of men every day. Its not just men and women, same sex partners adopt the sad old process too, with one being the woman and the other the bloke. They say women have a sixth sense; of course men will never know whether it's a myth or true, but what we do know is that even when we have done nothing wrong, we probably have and just don't know it!

Is this a chauvinistic point of view? Not intentionally, its just funny, and the more I have chatted with friends the more the subject raises a titter here and there. This book is a collection of examples drawn from self-inflicted grief; stories from friends and from watching complete strangers declare war on each other in public.

The following is written 'tongue in cheek', it will have some people outraged at the implied tarnishing of the female of the species, you may agree or disagree but treat it as an observation of life, yes from a male point of view, but oh so possibly true!

When I started thinking about a top 50 of those common phrases, words, subjects or questions, it was pretty clear that there are so many that link together it was going to be difficult to put them into an order; so the simplest way is to put them into sections and instead of a top 50 in order to just keep in separate chapters, after all they rarely come in one's, more often two's, three's and ten's don't they? Without intending to the actual count is nearer 60 but as some inclusions are similar to others so the total is probably nearer the 50 intended. The extras are a bonus for you, the reader.

If you recognise some the comments then you will understand where I am coming from, nod, snigger or pretend not to if someone is looking over your shoulder!

Words

Where to start? Why not simple words; words said in a certain way that mean so much more than their dictionary definition. Actually that's not a bad way of starting, alternative definitions, what the words might really mean.

Fine: (adjective) 1. It will do I suppose 2. Actually I'm pissed with you 3. Is that the best you can do 4. I hate it but I'm not gonna let you know just yet.

Don't you just hate it when you ask how the day went, how a woman is feeling or if they like something you have toiled over for the last three hours of your life? When a she says 'fine' a you know is everything is far from fine; it's an invitation to delve deeper and find out what is wrong and could quite as easily mean "ask me what is wrong?"

The word 'fine' normally comes out if you have been out all day, obviously enjoying yourself and doing 'men things', while your other half has had a boring day doing stuff that they would rather not do alone and then you have the audacity to come in ,full of the joys of life and ask how the day has gone.

Do you feel guilty? If you do her mission is accomplished and you are back in your place. Looking down at the floor is a good idea because you are on dodgy ground. If you say nothing get ready for a slice or two of 'nag pie' but on the other hand say something witty and you have had it too, you are damned if you do and damned if you don't.

So where do you go from here? You ask in an inquisitive and caring tone, "only fine?" That usually does the trick and what follows will probably be contained in this book, it certainly stands a chance.

***Morning: (noun)** 1. I'm still angry 2. I'm a grown up so I will be civil for a start 3. Don't think its all-better*
Now 'morning' with a smile is great but with a straight face and no eye contact it can make you feel like the nightmare is still going on even though you are awake now.

Picture the night before, a communication breakdown over a trivial matter and then after a restless night under the duvet you wake up and for a few seconds you feel rested and content. As you glance over into wide-open eyes you say something, and "morning" is the reply, closely followed by a sharp exit from the mattress and a flick of the duvet that nearly has your eye out. That sinking feeling returns, it's most definitely not fixed.

On the other hand you might meet in no-man's land, the kitchen or god forbid the bathroom, if one of you is already up. Kitchens are dangerous places, lots of sharp instruments and plates but the bathroom is probably worse, it's a personal place and with mirrors and reflective surfaces there is nowhere to hide! In this case 'morning' followed by a walk past is a combination that reinforces the message...all isn't quite right.

Silence: (verb) 1. Don't speak to me 2. Are you ready to apologise yet? 3. You really hurt me

OK not a spoken word but an action and boy, what a powerful one! Ever had the silent treatment? Bet you have, it ranks pretty high in the all time top 50, and in fact it might be number one.

Silence makes you feel bad or worse, is it a way of winding each other up? Is it something that mums pass onto daughters? No matter how many times it is used it still feels fresh and new, why is that?

For millennia men have struggled to find a way to deal with the silent treatment and have failed. They have tried to ignore it and treat silence with silence but in the end they blart something out and kick themselves for falling into the trap, "everything ok?" they ask and "fine" comes back...!

Of course these three little words are the start of the fun, we know it and women do too; the words used are the starter and the entrée is about to be served in the form of a question, which is the real day brightener.

Talking of day brighteners, don't be fooled by the false smile that is used with a comment. Saying something with a smile is reserved to the sales assistants of this world, not your partner and even when they say something with a smile it is best to check the shape of the smile and more importantly, if strained muscles are holding it in place. If, by chance it's a 'false smile' then it might be time to get your guard up because that sarcastic little comment is due any second.

Early Doors

There are insecurities in any relationship and if a man recognises the potential for big portions of 'nag pie' they can use the elbow, dispense with the offending person and seek out another one with less of an inclination for baking.

The honeymoon period has no time scale, some have it for years and years while others sadly get a few months bliss before it is gone forever.

During the honeymoon period partners become engrossed with each other, spending as much time as they can in each others company, declining a night out with the boys or girls, missing a golf match here and there and letting the subscription to the gym lapse for a month or two.

Rabbits have nothing on the bedroom antics and slowly the claws sink in deeper and a man is hooked, owned and managed. It happens all the time and we love it, but sometimes during that honeymoon period we get asked some questions and start to hear little comments that should be a warning sign. Do we do anything about it, no we don't so complaining is pointless later.

Why don't you want to see me later?

You have spent weekends living in each others pockets and then up pops a text asking you if you want a lads night out. Hmmm, what do you do?

Mark my words it's the start of things to come if you get the question, "why don't you want to se me?" Sometimes this question is coupled with cow eyes; thinking about it this is quite appropriate description for some. Cow eyes. The alternative are those big eyes that Puss in Boots uses in the Shrek films, they really add impact and how often do we fall for it.

What do we do? We text our mates back and take a

rain check with a lame excuse that the dog has just thrown up or your great uncle goober has arrived on the doorstep unexpectedly.

Oh, how cute, we could have a dog like that.

Maybe not a slice of pie but a warning if it is said in the first couple of weeks in a relationship!

A stroll in the park, stopping off at the grumpy ice cream van man, she chooses the same choc-ice as you do and comments "wow we even like the same ice cream!" Then a puppy runs past, as if possessed, and puts the anchors on to run back and sniff your leg before jumping up with muddy paws all over your jeans. Now if you boot it away you will be seen as a beast, so you raise a smile and she utters the immortal words "oh, how cute, we could have a dog like that" just to test you out.

What do you do? Yes you agree and fall into the trap, commitment!

This room would look good painted aubergine!

It's you pad, she has stopped over a few times, done that thing that you like under the bedclothes to cement the relationship, and now she wants to redecorate your living room due to the apparent lack of taste you have in pastel shades.

Homemaking, changing your pad to accommodate her taste, wrong, wrong, wrong!

Stuck between a rock and a hard place you might really like this one and quite enjoy the fact that you get to sleep in your own bed instead of at hers where the window is open and you can't decide whether to stay under the duvet or on top, cold then hot then cold equals no sleep. What do you do? Again you concede and head off to the Home Depot, B&Q in the UK, and stand in the paint aisle comparing colour charts before picking up a value roller set and disposable brushes. She has already cost you money for something you didn't even need to do! How did that happen?

I'm glad you like me.

Again, when said early in a relationship, this is a test to make you say more than 'like', they want to hear 'love' at the earliest opportunity. Maybe not the morning after the first night, but after a week or two it is expected that you declare your undying 'love'.

Perhaps I should have defined 'love' as a word in the first part of the chapter but here lies the problem, it is a really powerful and meaningful word and so shouldn't be used lightly. You have to mean it not just say it to avoid the cold shoulder treatment. In your teens you broadcast it at the earliest opportunity, you tell your mum that you "love her" after a few hours of going out with her and even if your mother thinks she isn't good enough for you, you don't care. After the first day or two of the relationship texting the word or saying it on the phone you say, "love you" at every opportunity again and again. It is repeated during the 'hang up' game, recognise this crazy performance? "You hang up first", "you still there?", "ok together then, one, two three.... are you there still?"... "mwah, love you."

What do we all do, we say 'love' to please, but as you get older it becomes a word like banana if your not careful, a throwaway word, just like the fruit when it goes brown. It starts to have meaning when you meet 'the one' or you have kids, but even then word is used to placate and reassure your partner instead of you really meaning the true definition, whatever it really is.

If you have been bitten by the love bug and have been let down with a failed relationship you can find it harder to say, until you get trapped again into saying it. Will we ever learn?

Where did you get that?

Although men are capable of buying trinkets for their own pad, women find this house-making a bizarre concept with a preconception that men are not capable of going to the department store and shop for a an ornament or painting. Because of this preconception they assume that we must have bought it with another woman previously and so starts the inquisitive approach to find out where the Monet print or the three elephants carved from finest mahogany that adorn the display cabinet came from. The secondary questioning further casts doubt on your design prowess to place the little heffalumps in a row, just like the ones in the Jungle Book, aww, cute but clearly a woman's touch…which one?

"That's nice where did you get that" is followed by a statement, "suppose you bought it with her." If you come down one morning and find the elephants stuffed into a drawer then don't be surprised.

So how many have you slept with then?

The number question, oh my days! Why is it such an important question? Don't answer is the best option, closely followed by a statement that "you don't do numbers thank you".

If for some reason you do keep count then isn't it better to keep it a closely guarded secret? Apart from the fact that it is a personal thing, think about the implications of the admission, especially if you big it up and add a few to the true number. It may backfire, you might get asked names, rating out of ten and locations! By the way, lads do big it up, it's a testosterone thing, conquests and blagging rights so even if they do say a number it is probably baloney.

It can also lead to a slice of 'nag pie' years later with the numerical admission thrown back during an argument, "I suppose the thirty you had before me were better!" what the heck! While on the subject it is probably not a good idea to rank the current one halfway, lie and let her know she is the best, ever!

Another reason not to go into numbers is if a man says X and the woman says Y, which is double X, this can lead to invisible 'nag pie' with the man giving himself a hard time for not beating her record. On top of this insecurity the male mathematical mind kicks in and doing long division with the 'total quoted' divided by the 'common denominator', being active years of sexual activity, and an answer beyond belief. Further male questioning might bring out an unwanted answer, that to achieve such a high number the total included the occasional doubling up, i.e. two at a time!

It's safe to say that avoiding the question is the best policy and with the references to 'early doors' complete the obvious next stage is to look at the things that couples do together that leads to 'nag pie.' When talking about the things that couples do I am not referring to 'that thing' that starts off well until the relationship blossoms, a ring goes on a finger, vows are said and living together becomes a routine.

From nowhere tiredness, stress and headaches kick in and where there was once unlimited access a press stud miraculously appears or a piece of Velcro, is invisibly darned in place.

That's a nice name for a boy/girl

Run Forrest run! If after a few weeks this one comes out you have been selected as a donor, a mate and provider so unless you feel the same get the heck out of there!

On the other hand she might just come out with, "do you see yourself with kids?" Kids with her that is, not the ones from two previous marriages.

Choosing baby names brings a whole new chapter to your life, and not wanting to offend any reader I am not going to quote a name or two here as examples...well maybe I will just for fun.

The classic is the celebrity name, to copy a child born into the world with rich parents and a distinct lack of discretion. Naming a child after the place of conception comes to mind but drawing the line at Bognor, with a middle name Regis, has to be made. Any suggestion that your own child is named after a city that you have never visited should be rejected out of principle.

The same goes for a name that you hear shouted across the supermarket at a naughty kid that keeps opening the Haribos; there is nothing worse that a screeching brummie voice shouting at Scarlet with a threat to 'tan her backside' if she doesn't behave. You know the kid is in trouble when you hear "Scarlet Carmen Smith, get here now!" Poor Scarlet, I bet Clark Gable would be turning in his grave if he knew that his Southern Beau's namesake would gravitate to a naughty kid, embarrassed by her mum in Tesco.

Surely you need to see the new-born in the flesh before deciding what to call him or her. It makes sense to take into account the surname and proposed first name combination to avoid years of grief for the poor child. Don't fall into the trap, however intentional, that Mr and Mrs Tools did when naming Jennifer who probably went through school with a nickname after shortening her name to Jenny, Jenny Tools. Or poor Thomas Arto who probably had a nickname after shortening his name to Tom Arto. Last but no means least is Samuel Wedge, will probably had references to BLT's or tuna and sweet corn through his childhood, Sam Wedge; OK one more for luck, to the 'Richard's' of this world with Ball as a surname, good call Mr and Mrs Ball. You can work that one out yourself.

Back to the 'nag pie'; now if and when names are discussed the joint decision is often a majority vote, after all she has carried the little bundle for nine months and has first dibs on the preferred name. If a man wants to risk 'nag pie' conceding the first given name may be prudent and getting the second given name as a compromise might be a great trade off.

For most, thankfully, baby name choosing coincides with a respite in 'nag pie' baking, probably due to the bilious feeling and hormone imbalance that prevents regular contact with baking ingredients. Overall it is a joyous period in a relationship, where the experience is one to savour. Fun shopping for a pram, wallpaper, cot and baby clothes is actually a delight. Proud dads-to-be look at baby size football kits as well as the bunny baby grows and mum's with maternity jeans long for the day they will fit into the dozen pairs of size ten's hanging redundant in the wardrobe.

Not that the nine months is pie free, there will be a slice or two if she wants reassurance that she is still beautiful and not fat so don't make the mistake of bringing up 'space hoppers' into the conversation when reminiscing about you favourite toys when you were eight.

With this in mind moving on to normal shopping is appropriate now, and the next chapter will certainly ring a few bells to many a man, warning bells!

2
Shopping

Man's worst enemy, we can't do right for doing wrong whether it's the weekly supermarket trolley push or the shopping mall we are always at risk. Just one innocuous comment or facial expression away from a slice of pie! Here's the thing, no matter how hard we try and show willing on a shopping trip we are two seconds away from ruining the day without even knowing it.

Let's get something straight here, men go shopping, pick something up and pay for it; they are done, well maybe 99% of the time. They can be in and out before the one hour parking charge clicks over into the two hour rate, whereas a couple can spend a whole day window shopping and buying the same stuff. It's often a recipe for disaster.

All starts well, even if we are wound up with the backseat driver pointing out the empty spaces that we have ignored on purpose, before **we** park the car where **we** want to, thank you. A delightful cuppa and a bun at the coffee shop should be the foundation for a wonderful day fulfilling the list of items discussed in the car on the way to the shops.

How often does the list miraculously grow though? Items never discussed find their way into the basket, more that likely the invisible ink used on the list. Expecting to spend a few notes, it soon becomes clear that this might turn into the shopping spree of the decade. This is probably an appropriate the time to call the credit card company and increase the limit, just in case.

Clothes' shopping is probably the most volatile thing a couple can do, although home improvement and furniture shopping rank a close second.

Believe it or not men expect to be lured into the shopping experience, which includes lots of questions designed to test them to the extreme. Loaded questions and testing comments, to respond to the satisfaction of their partner or it can quickly ruin a day.

Does this look good?
"No you look like a bag of spuds!"

Referring to her looking like a bag of spuds may seem like a genuine answer but probably not the best one to use.

No matter how tempting it is to reply with this sarcastic gem the truth is that when men hear this it sends a chill through their bones. It might be an innocent question asked for an honest opinion, but it's a loaded question.

Think about it, if a piece of clothing has been picked up and tried on she thinks it will suit her. She likes it and is looking for reassurance that it looks great. Be very careful here, honesty isn't always the best policy. If a man says 'yes', but does it just to get a move on to get back for the football on the telly, they run the risk of being quoted later at home when their woman tries it on again. Say 'no' then better be prepared to explain why it looks rubbish, with a constructive and politically correct reply!

Which one do you prefer?
"Neither they both look rank!"

'Rank' is a bit harsh here so perhaps "they don't

flatter your voluptuous curves" might work better on reflection.

Oh no, a choice! Of course it could be a way of getting a man to say, "buy them both" but lets not be too negative shall we. It isn't as simple as saying "that one" because men know they will need to explain why the 'other one' isn't as flattering.

Choosing one isn't actually your decision in the end, and even if it isn't the right one there is a chance that you will find the item hidden away in the future, in the wardrobe, labels on!

I haven't got a pair that colour!

"No sweetheart you haven't, the other four pairs you have are only slightly newer and a hint of a shade darker!"

Of course this assumes that you pointlessly keep count of the pile of leather stuffed into the wardrobe or under the stairs. Think about it, she wants them and even if you think it's a bit of overkill the decision has probably been made already. Offering a logical reason to avoid duplication will fall on deaf ears, jeez. Forget the rationale it's a want thing so go with it.

Besides that, what do men know about fashion items? We don't read glossy mags, well we might do but that's not important right now, we don't read Vogue or Take a Break, unless we are in the dentists waiting room, honest! When we do though we see the same glossy and tempting image as our woman and we also see the designer outfit that the editor has sourced on the High Street at a fraction of the price, but that's not important either, she wants to look like a celebrity. Get the card out and stop whinging.

40% off, these are in the sale, bargain!
"Maths was never your strongest subject at school was it?"

Here we go time to explain …you will pay 60% for the privilege, so how the heck is that saving money? Wasted words! You might as well offer a theory on Pythagoras instead of simple 'fractions revision' because it will go straight over her head too.

Unless the 'sale item' is something that was on the shopping list it becomes an extra item and no matter how much you might think it is a luxury to buy it you might as well button your lip and let her feel it is a bargain. Just agree and move on, 60% lighter

On a positive note five items at 40% off equate to three at full price so at least the wardrobe will have more items per square inch, less space for more, bonus! Actually forget that because you nicely spaced suit rack may all of a sudden have a few foreign items appear next to them. Your shirts may be destined to be forever creased and crumpled, until you buy another wardrobe that is!

Do you want anything?
"Why would I want to extend the shopping trip any more than necessary?"

Is this reverse psychology and a way justifying the overspending spree? Perhaps, but even if you say 'yes' then be prepared to have items picked up and held against you even if you can't stand the look of them. God forbid that you reject every suggestion and if you do then expect a "you never try anything on that I like" comment. This leads on quite nicely to having clothes chosen for you, sometimes to keep you looking young even though a fashion guru has designed them for teenagers and twenty something's. Yes she might want you to look like the bronzed Adonis, that swept her off her feet many years ago or that young stud in the office, and perhaps as she approaches her prime the thought of you now twenty years past your prime is something that can be fixed with new clothes.

Men grow old too quickly, yes, probably due to the overeating on 'nag pie' in part, but years of a regular pint or two can play havoc with the mid section and even if the clothes do suit, the bulge just above the belt isn't a good look with a tight tee shirt clinging to it.

Birthdays and Christmas bring an opportunity to have a wrapped pressie presented to you at stupid o'clock when your senses haven't woken up and the mulled wine has given you a right old thick head. Opening the paper to see a nicely folded top with the question, "do you like it?" results in the cliché answer, "just what I wanted" through clenched teeth. Yes you do like it, its 'fine' although you know you will face ridicule when your mates see you wearing it.

At the same time, the pressie you spent hours looking for, because you have bought her everything she needed in normal shopping trips for the previous 12 months, is unwrapped and the response of your very own question to whether you have done well this year is, "yes it's nice." Hope you kept the receipt, roll on the turkey, time for a bucks fizz even though it's 7am.

I would add that this anecdote has nothing to do with the wonderful pressie's I have received in the past, clothes that fit and thankfully the bulge isn't apparent so looking like a younger man worked, thank you. Shame the dress sense made no difference to being traded in for a younger model though.

In addition the pressies that I have given have hopefully been received with a little more enthusiasm than 'fine.' Clearly my guilt has generated a disclaimer requirement and thus as it is now committed to text, the whole reference made without prejudice, just in case the lawyers want to use it!

Why can't we afford it?
"Because the credit card is maxed out and we haven't planned to buy this!"

Justifying a big spend is something that, for lot's of couples, is a joint decision but occasionally when one says "no we can't afford that" the other will ask why. After all it isn't that expensive and you should be able to afford it! The counter argument may refer to two salaries, surely her money is hers to spend, not for bills, how rude.

I blame Maggie Thatcher, well not the Baroness in person but the government of the time. The era and advent of 'buy now pay later' during the 1980's with store credit cards for the masses gave us spending power. This new power convinced many of us 'then teenagers' to spend wages on going out and, when the cash was low, to pop into Fosters or Burtons to buy that acrylic ski jumper, tucked in of course to pinstripe tight jeans, very fashionable, Ooh, and an extra pair of leg warmers and then charge the lot to the Sears Card. At, something like, 29% APR, we bought on the drip.

Access and Barclaycard lost the lead and we applied for other credit cards that took the place of that 'something for the weekend space' in wallets. This education of a generation brainwashed millions into keeping a balance on the card and only paying the minimum every month, genius! The net result was that couples started with debt and then added to the balance with items for the home, items needed now not later.

When it came to clothes, ahh! just add it to the debt, we will pay it off one day. The problem is that some realised the trap and getting out of it generated a boom in home baking, more pies than ever before were being served up with the main ingredient 'affordability' and a few drops of 'essence of common sense'.

Is it any wonder that the same generation has more divorces than previous generations? The trouble is that after selling up the family home and splitting the equity, the debts may have been paid off but both are out there looking for mister or missus right. Off they go back to the retro 80's club night after years away. Singles enter the cattle market and in an attempt to be noticed and to lure and attract, they are whacking new clothes on a card, hopefully ones that fit well of course. The cycle continues and you have to laugh or you would cry!

New couples in their 30's and 40's re-join the 'game of slice' and with time running out in their careers, building a big pension pot usually means that this is the last chance to make that promotion in the salad years. Work is therefore a place that causes 'alternative views' and the next chapter looks at the work place and the ever present 'nag pie' potential.

3
Work

Wherever you work and whatever you do for a living, work can cause the occasional misunderstanding. Getting in late from work for a legitimate reason is treated with some doubt and the following comments ooze out as part of the indirect questioning.

Over dinner moaning about work can lead to a slice of 'nag pie' for desert. Comments like ...

Why do you let your boss speak to you like that?
Which is more closer to being asked directly "are you a man or a mouse?"

There is nothing more condescending if your partner thinks you are a wimp when your boss puts demands on you. Here's the thing, you might feel that you are being hard done by however you know how to deal with pressure because you live it for nine hours a day. The last thing you need is having your partner add to the frustration even if her motive is to enthuse you.

Did you ask?
This probably leads on from a conversation over last night's lasagne when you were fired up to address a grievance and the easy option yesterday was to agree with her to kick some bottoms, hell yes. However after a night's sleep and the commute to work this fire in your belly has all but gone out and

you talk yourself out of the confrontation. What a lightweight!

It is always simple for the person not facing the boss to egg you along and load the bullets, if you don't fire the gun you might as well turn it on yourself in truth.

Why can't you leave it at work?

"Thanks for the support honey, just sharing my day with you and having a moan, but if you don't give a damn then I will clam up!"

Women take an interest when it suits, so do men in truth, but the old adage of expecting your woman to just 'listen' is certainly going out of fashion, especially with both men and women chucking in 40 hours a week to keep the income up, for shopping! The other way round though expect to let her blow off steam about Hilda being late for work, again, and that she left early for another dental appointment. Bloody liberty, just agree... "Ooh, I know" said in the style of Sybil Fawlty!

The Office Do

There are two types of 'Work Do', the one with partners and the 'Office Do' with definitely **no** partners.

Either way the annual party has the potential of lots of fallout before, during and after or can lead to more than a slice of 'nag pie.' As far as which is worse, well this depends on lots of things, but the main problem for the one where you both attend is your work persona and your home persona. How often do people act a certain way at work and are different at home? It never ceases to amaze me how different some people are, confident in their job but complete whooses when their partner is around.

I am not saying that the cocky knob that always cracks innuendos and flirts uncontrollably with every female is a shadow of himself at home, but it stands a chance. Yes people flirt at work, and very occasionally the flirt turns into something more, if both accept the advances and graduate from a fumble in the stationary cupboard to full-blown sex on the boardroom table...sorry almost digressed into that erotic prose again! But that's the point it is fiction for almost every workplace, whereas couples imagine that it takes place all day every day, if he says hello to her he must be shagging her, clearly.

Maybe this distrust is the catalyst for some innocent liaisons to progress and perhaps after a few slices of the 'nag pie' some just say, "sod it" and have a play because they are being accused anyway.

Of course those that 'do' cause those that 'don't' immense grief, let alone the poor people actually involved in affairs.

What makes it worse is seeing co-workers having a play and then, out of disgust, taking the flabbergasted thoughts home to share; then before you know it... you are at it as well! Is it any wonder secrets are kept? Self preservation comes to mind.

Wow, serious stuff! So lets leave the adulterers adulteresses to their own guilt trip and thank them for putting the seed of doubt in the innocents' lives. Cheers for that.

Back to the office party with your partner in tow, on show or ready to give you a blow...with a blunt instrument that is, not the other thing, which has probably stopped now anyway and is a distant memory. Here are a few classic phrases that many of us have heard before, and will hear again no doubt.

You never told me that

Normally pops out in conversation with someone saying something about what happened in the office last week. It can be a regurgitated account of what you said to a colleague, which had the office in hysterics at the time, but you forgot to say anything at home. The moment had passed after all and you 'had to be there'. That is why you failed to mention it at home! Oops. This can lead to that feeling of guilt and even if it was a small thing it will be made out to be something far bigger on the way home, you just know it.

What he meant to say was ...

What's that all about, whether it's at a party with friends or the office bash, where was the invitation to speak for me and worse correct me in front of other people?

Are men incapable of communicating or does the fact that we don't communicate properly with women mean that women can act as our translator without our permission or blessing?

Yes we may say stupid things but men understand this and probably don't care what we have just said, unless we have called their wife a moose. When we say something like "yes the weekend away was alright, food was a bit dodgy but is was a nice break" this gets translated into, "what he meant to say was that WE had a really relaxing break, fine wine, fine food and even though it was overcast we managed to spend time in the shops and doing a bit of sightseeing." Sounds great, wish I had been there!

Another rough translation that rears its ugly head on occasion is the one-upmanship to big up something in front of others. The cosy house we have just moved into becomes a five-bedroom mansion with the small utility room classed as an extra room or the walk in wardrobe a converted master bedroom. This twisted piece of truth is however easily spotted when your colleague picks you up the day your car is in for a service and he then realises that the mansion is really a four-bed link detached. It can be a little confusing when they pull into the road initially and wonder how and where a larger house would fit into the standard Lego houses either side of the road.

So, when you partner speaks for you it is probably best to let it flow because you might find some amusement in the alternate universe you must live in.

Who's she?

Introducing the new credit controller, who moonlights as a part time glamour model, is always a sticky moment especially when the office juniors and the recently divorced MD are blatantly pouring over her trying to get her attention, their jaws by their belly buttons.

For those of us in a healthy, loving and trusting relationship the anticipation of something being said is often too great for us to cope with and so maybe we say something, or maybe we don't.

It is made worse if you interviewed her and were part of the decision to employ her over the 50 year old with one eye and lumbago, with similar qualifications. The assumption that you must fancy her outweighs the fact that she was the best candidate. If you mentioned her in passing over dinner a month ago but played down her stunning looks and ample chest then you deserve a slice of pie.

However nice 'she' is, 'she' will be a tart in your lover's eyes and so introducing the other half to the Amazon Woman will likely lead to an uncomfortable situation.

She's attractive
"Who, her?"

The new Sales Director who you never come into contact with. The question is a test to see what you say, if you say 'yes' then you obviously fancy her if you say 'no' and she is a pretty woman then you are a lying git.

The reality is probably that 'she' is happily married with two kids at private school and is a career woman. In your professional capacity you enjoy a pleasant but plutonic working relationship. Do you heck, to your partner she is clearly a threat, and even if she is the bitch from hell at work you must have tried it on, after all you are a bloke. What a crock!

You left me alone

"Oh I'm sorry I didn't realise that you are incapable of mingling with my work mates, that being said it doesn't seem to stop you when you are out and about with strangers, developing that false laugh and a flick of the hair!"

It's likely that leaving your partner with a one of your team is dangerous; they could be an axe murderer for all she knows. Of course some people we work with are dead boring, or just dead from the neck up, and leaving your lady with one of them on purpose is a bit naughty, but fun none the less.

The other danger of leaving your partner with fellow workers is that she might vent her frustration with the wrong person if they mention the paltry pay rise or possible job cuts. There she goes speaking for you again. Another danger is that in the strained social conversation that your secretary mentions the forthcoming trip to Dubai that you haven't had the opportunity to share with your partner yet because it coincides with a wedding, on her side of the family of course, or you anniversary.

Is this why we try and stay glued to our partners as much as possible, just in case we say or they hear something that has been missed over the dinner table, in the last year?

In fact this leads on nicely to the next question concerning working away.

You're off abroad again then?

For some working away in far away places, in this country or even for a night or two during the week, can generate a buffet tableful of pies to choose from.

Being away and fasting from home made 'nag pie' is often a cycle of returning to gluttony and eating huge portions when you get back home. The questioning starts when you get back on what you did while you were away. Forget the fact that you are overseas and trying to please your employers so that the salary gets paid at the end of the month; being away is obviously a holiday with drunken debauchery every night, especially with the attractive Sales Director there, the tart!

The reality however is far from the image presented to you; airport lounges, delays, hotel rooms that bring on claustrophobia, early starts having to talk to nauseous people at breakfast followed by 12 hour days and a two hour seat in the restaurant to get served a meal that stays within the expenses guideline. Yes that really equates to back scuttling someone you meet in the bar after a day on a sun lounger by the pool, doesn't it. Because of the perception of a working holiday, when it comes round to announcing the next trip men often wait for the opportune moment to mention it and if this doesn't present itself beforehand the office party can let the cat out of the bag just in time for Christmas. Enjoy your Yule log won't you.

How did he/she get a promotion over you?
If you recently missed out on a promotion then come the office party your honey will be out to find out who beat you to the position. When you enter the function her radar will fix on the git who beat you and the mission is afoot; she will want to speak to them and make it difficult in the form of a subliminal slice of pie. Poor sod.

It will stand a chance that the newly promoted person will be a little more relaxed this year as their climb to the next rung of the ladder is complete and so they might let their hair down a bit more than normal, just to show the staff that they are a fun person too. This will play into your other halves hands beautifully and when golden nuts comes out with some drivel they will likely pounce and make a cutting remark, just to put them in their place.

No matter what happens at the party, on the way home get ready for the character assignation of your work mates, after all they are 'your friends, not hers' If you are not careful questions of your ability compared to the Muppet who won promotion will be a painful experience.

Is it any wonder that fewer and fewer couples attend the office party nowadays? Surely it can't be coincidence that more companies have a staff party with no partners compared to previous years. Cut backs are not the real reason, are they?

This possible change of party policy has fuelled the fire in the oven allowing for new recipes of 'nag pie' to be tried out. The new recipes are similar to the usual pies that you get from going out with your friends. This delightful tasting pie is called the cross-examination pie, which happens to be the next chapter.

4
Cross Examination

Any barrister or QC will have the art of cross-examination of a witness down to a tee. Women can fire a sequenced list of questions at a man and find the answer they are looking for, not the truth perhaps but the answer they want to hear.

The answers a man gives are used as evidence, sometimes years later and when a man hears "you said" they know that a statement made is going to be regurgitated and entered into the conversation, with a few tweaks of course.

Questioning usually starts with a standard question like "how was your day?" or "how was you night?" and depending on the answer there are probably some of these questions stacked up behind.

What time did you come in?
Make sure you know exactly what time you stumbled in because she already knows, even if she was fast asleep, how do women do that?

Of course the lateness of the hour is an indication of how much unauthorised fun you have had, to be used in a later discussion. Your answer and the time are filed away for next week when she arrives home at 4am and you, quite rightly ask the same question over breakfast, or maybe brunch. Her sore head and hangover might generate an answer like this, "well you barged in at 3.30am last week making a racket!"

Bet you are glad you asked, 1:0 down and an own goal.

Who did you see?

Another one that really means, "What did you get up to?" Replying with "no one really" is suicide. Let's face it you **must** have seen someone, anyone, so 'nobody' translates to obviously someone you don't want to tell her you saw.

Apart from the fact that if you had a belly full of ale you probably won't remember EVERYONE you saw in the room. The only option is to make notes on your phone just in case, but after a few drinks it is likely to read Stoofen instead of Steve so make sure you use spell check, or recognise the Enigma code used.

Keeping a running log in your head of what time you spoke to might be the answer but if you spout a rehearsed monologue it will sound fishy, so try and avoid, "1027 hours saw John, approached him at 1028 hours, passing Jenny but ignored her due to the crowds; 1031 hours John and I spoke briefly to two women, didn't get their names but have seen them in the playground before... 1036 hours went for a number one, considered a number two but toilet seat was drenched already..."

Was he/she there?

Oh lord, one of your mates she hates! A perfectly innocent human that she doesn't like for some reason. Traitor! Did you fail by being courteous and saying hello and do you admit it, even though there is nothing in it?

Here's the thing men try to get on with people and 99% of the time it is an innocent conversation, nothing in it, but from nowhere nodding across a room is tantamount to a quickie in the fire exit!

You look guilty!

"That's probably because your looking at me with those dilated pupils that are trying to read my mind. Have you not heard of innocent until proven guilty, or it is that Jedi Mind Trick you are trying out again, to catch me out, even when I have done nothing wrong?"

Where does this comment come from and how does my smiling face clearly mean I have robbed a bank when I popped to the cashpoint? An infuriating phrase that probably makes us really look guilty and in an attempt to disguise our annoyance it makes it worse as we go 0-60 inside for being accused of something that we haven't done, again.

Woe betide you

Now my old headmaster said this to all the kids in my infants school (that's year's one or two in new money) and it put the fear of god into me when I was seven; but hearing it again in adult life is farcical. What is the punishment then detention or expulsion from the marriage?

It's a veiled threat, which means 'if I catch you out, you've had it.' It almost makes you want to make up a confession just to avoid the secret punishment that might happen if you are caught out from something you haven't done. It conjures up a picture of Dickensian life, indeed the phrase is probably from the 1800's, a time when thirty lashes of the birch were considered a mild penalty compared to a long trip to Australia on a ship? Bet she would love to see you get the lashes though, the minx!

You might as well tell the truth now

"As opposed to lying, oh wait a minute I am telling the truth already."

What is this something out of Braveheart? Do I now do my best Mel Gibson impression and with a Scottish twang shout "FREEDOM" or admit my so called sins to save the pain of that sharp pointy implement that you will gouge my entrails out with? Oh, and while I am at it I may as well pledge allegiance to the King, the Long-shanker or is it allegiance to you, the Queen?

You know

"I know what, that your creative mind has dreamt something up? Actually I really don't know but give me a hint?"

But we don't, that's the whole point. Perhaps we should but when Neanderthal man changed into Homo Sapiens he was absent the day they taught mind reading, sorry about that.

If there are aliens out there and they have telepathic skills, I really hope that they cross a galaxy or three and head for Earth with a view to passing on the powers to us blokes, then we would be able to decipher this ambiguous statement without any risk of misinterpreting it, and be on the same telepathic level as women. Bliss!

I know, you know

"Wonderful, so you know that I know, or is that don't know because I have absolutely no idea what you know that I know."

On the other hand if you already know then why are you asking? If then I know you know, then haven't I done my bit in letting you know, so why are you telling me you know? Ah it's because you want to let me know that you know so if I now say I don't know it's irrelevant, that will be it, you know. It makes perfect sense now, so again, what are you actually saying?

I can see it in your eyes

"What, a reflection of insecurity? Or have you a special skill to read my mind through my retina? If you can what am I thinking about now? Yes correct, Get a grip woman."

Where in time did women learn to read a man through his eyes? Unless we are on to body language and inaccuracies with what comes out of our mouths versus to leaning backwards or forwards, glancing to the ceiling to avoid the piercing glare and in turn saying something else. Some of it might be true but overall let's face it you cant see anything 'in our eyes' can you?

We'll see

"What are we back to the eye thing or is this something different?"

This is another throwaway comment that reeks of what she knows that you know as well. Time will tell eh, so let's see if I trip up in 2018 and say something to contradict what you just said, I will then be guilty by default, brilliant.

What it does is to put the gauntlet down for a future discussion, perhaps in the summing up after further cross examination, so yes let's see shall we.

You said ...

Ahh the summing up, like any good legal eagle, using evidence to implicate and demonstrate to the judge, who happens to be the prosecutor as well by the way, that you are guilty, guilty I say!

There is nothing worse than having what you said repeated back to you but with the words in a different order that says something else. We are back to the translation again. When a man says "didn't see anyone really" and then after a few more minutes in the dock they mention that they saw Jade with her friends in the queue when he came out, within seconds she pounces, "but you said you didn't see anyone, but you saw that harlot Jade, so who else have you forgotten to mention?" is thrust in your direction, "ha gotcha!"

We are back on memory loss, short-term memory losses in truth. Men don't intentionally forget things, it's just that some things are just not important to us; they are to women, but not to us.

Only through conversation will something trigger one of these short-term flashbacks and when we then say something we are accused of hiding something, bizarre. Thankfully every day conversations don't warrant a debrief by MI5.' One government cutback men support.

Did you ask?

"No I didn't, nor any other off the wall questions that are nothing to do with what I am telling you."

It's almost as if, under cross-examination, she has prepared a load of questions that she will ask if you asked.

One after another the suggested questions are read back to you and before you can think you start to feel totally stupid that you didn't think to ask the obvious question or series of questions. Until you realise that the questions that you should have asked, in her opinion, are not that applicable. Stop putting words into my mouth, argh!

What is that smell?

Ranks alongside the lipstick on the collar observation, which has no defence at all and deserves a couple of pies to be consumed simultaneously.

A woman's nose is one of her most sensitive senses and she can smell perfume on a man from ten paces. Let's face it if you have the misfortune to brush past a woman, that works at a department store in the perfume section and adopts the bottle a night principle, the odds of getting a transfer of scent increase dramatically. Alternatively one of the lads might have gone overboard on the Eau de Toilette and the particular fragrance of choice this month is that girly floral effort that makes your sandalwood based aftershave seem like a spray of water.

A night on the town means mingling with more smells than a bloodhound will encounter in it's life and inevitably your clothes, washed by your partners fair hand using the jasmine softener, will adopt a new aroma. This being said the presence of a fruity bouquet is probably going to arose some suspicion and can be the catalyst for a cross examination to end all cross examinations.

For the innocents among us we should pay homage to the over perfumed women that frequent bars and clubs and have the annoying habit of dousing themselves in public with another coat of body spray; thank you.

After a night out on the town, the weekend might hold the pleasure or home improvement, chores and tasks that you have been putting off for a month or two. In the trade off of receiving a 'pass' to go out your commitment to DIY means that hangover aside, your weekend is sure to include time together improving the home. The next chapter covers the joy of DIY

5

DIY – in fact, why don't you do it yourself then!

Home improvement, gardening and putting the bins out are part of the man routine; it also provides the perfect opportunity for men to react to being questioned on what they are doing. Women know this and if something isn't just right it is a real chance to get one or two comments in.

While some couples have a wonderful time working together, decorating and keeping their mansion in pristine condition the majority adopt the approach that the man does and the woman 'DIRECTS'!

For some reason women adopt the gaffer role at home and instead of letting men fix and finish the task they oversee the project and have the ability to come in at the exact time when a man is struggling with a task.

Flat Packed

What a great invention, furniture in a box and assembled at home under the watchful eye of the gaffer. Wouldn't men just love to reply to the clichés with some of these little beauties?

Did you follow the instructions?
"No, I decided to ignore the quick set up guide and guess what screw goes where!"

Whether you have the ability to follow the one sheet quick guide or rely on the three volumes of instructions, the one thing that men do is follow the instructions but sometimes we fix things together and something is missing. It's normally the poorly written instructions of course, but to question us really doesn't help ladies.

Should it look like that?
"Well obviously not because the picture is evidence enough that it isn't the same, oh I'm sorry you're referring to the lack of doors that I haven't put on yet, stupid me."

One thing men have worked out is that glossy pictures are not the real thing, they are photo shopped and created by photographers using proper lighting to entice you to buy. The replica, on the photo, is also a hand made imposter, not a real flat pack from aisle 6B, the image is one with with perfectly measured panels selected from the best grain wood and assembled with no gaps, unlike your one, that is a millimetre or two out.

The comparison of our effort to the brochure one is therefore not always an even playing field.

Oh look you haven't used all the bits.
"Yes that's the spare dowel that inadvertently crept into the bag when the IKEA man flat packed the monstrosity, shame he can't count isn't it."

Although things have improved with the computer driven bag packing of a number seven screw or a short dowel, sometimes an extra item creeps in. Point conceded if a panel of wood is left over but screws and connectors are a bonus in any man's book, spares for the Tupperware box that we collect raw plugs, nails and screws in. The extras you are hoarding for the secret project of building a coffin to bury your loved one in, bah rumbled!

It looks nothing like the one in the store.

"Well actually it does but it is now in our dingy place not in the open plan superstore, without ceilings and surrounded by things we don't own, and that's what the difference is."

The ones in the store have been put together by a highly trained assembler as well, probably from the Nordic Region and privy to skills passed down since the days of the Vikings from father to son. Even though we, men, would love to have these skills we are not all furniture makers, chippy's or can make up for the hole that is 3mm off centre courtesy of the underpaid factory worker that spends their day drilling thousands of holes into softwood panels.

Brush Strokes

Decorating the home is something that should bring a sense of achievement for a couple, the amateur attempt at creating a show home that would look good in a magazine.

Sometimes the efforts are questioned and for the paint splattered male with beads of sweat from working in a confined space for hours or days, these gems below are the last thing he wants to hear. Which is why he would love to reply with a sarcastic reply, if he had the balls to that is.

It looks darker
"That's because it hasn't dried yet!"

How many times have you painted a wall with magnolia or plum emulsion and as soon as it is on the wall the concern is shown? Yes, I too have been there and experienced the sense of foreboding that despite the colour chart and joint decision, I have picked up the wrong can of paint. Thankfully most of the time the colour on the can appears like magic when the wall has dried. Clever that!

Oh...you missed a bit
"It's the first coat, but thank you!"

Even with the advent of one coat paint it stands a chance that you will have missed a few square millimetres and short of chucking the contents on the wall, as if you were rinsing the car off with a bucket of water, explaining the observation with confidence that you have the process completely under control is the best policy.

On the other hand the bit you have missed might actually be the bit where she started painting an hour ago before disappearing to do something more important, so the bit I missed is actually the bit you missed.

Not sure if I like it
"Great, just finished, taken three hours and you prefer the terracotta. Joy!"

It happens, and worst of all the recently finished wall might require three coats of the lighter, revised colour choice; but at least its another thin protective layer on the plaster or wallpaper and another barrier to the elements and day-to-day spills and bumps.

There's a bubble under the wallpaper
"That will be the paste that needs to dry out so stop pushing your boney finger into it!"

Mini roller in your hand, resist the temptation to insert it into someone's nostril and show willing, casually walking over to the odd bulbous growth you give the bubble a little push, as if you know what you are doing. Then spend a few hours sweating just in case your paste appraisal is incorrect. Cross your fingers and hope that the bubble shrinks into oblivion and the wallpaper finds its way to the surface, reunited with the plaster again. If in the end the wallpaper sags, like someone's chest you know, expect a, "told you it wasn't right, idiot."

Are you happy with it?
"Well I was until you said that."

Another testing question, answer at you peril. Say 'yes' and it might show that your DIY skills are just not good enough to placate the judgmental eye of the gaffer; say 'no' and you have just volunteered to have another go. Better luck next time, and the next more than likely.

Gardening
Keeping the garden beautiful requires regular maintenance and while couples share the joy of maintaining the flowerbeds and lush grass together, often the man is allocated the garden as a trade off for the cleaning inside the house. From the upstairs window vantage point this is an ideal place to issue instructions from as she dusts the window ledge in between the first and second coat of nail varnish. To the amusement of the neighbours basking in the garden on their loungers they too share the comments.

Grass needs cutting
"Really? Yes, your right it has grown all of half an inch since last week."

It really is a wonderful thing grass, it grows when the rain falls or the sun shines, but occasionally a dry spell slows the miracle of growth. Explaining the botanical theory might not help here so a quick once over often satisfies, even with the blades set higher just for a laugh.

Can you make sure you keep the lines straight this time?
"Don't worry honey I will measure the distance between cuts and pay attention this time instead of wandering off at an angle just to wind you up! That would be obtuse."

Now if your lawn is to feature on the cover of Home and Garden then your lines will require exact pinpoint accuracy, but if the kids are going to play football or badminton later a wiggly line makes no difference. Your decision.

Did you mean to prune so many branches off?
"Actually no I became obsessed with the pruning shears and couldn't help myself, probably the vision of snipping your arms off sent me doolally. I can stick a few back on if you like my darling!"

'If it is overgrown butcher it,' this is the unwritten rule that men use for gardening, unless they have aspirations to exhibit at Chelsea next year.

Men are destructive and take pleasure in cutting back the herbaceous growth to save them doing it again next year. If women realised this it would be so much easier.

We have no idea really except that if we are cute and cut back too far it stands a chance that we will be able to dig it out and save time next growing season.

Are you going to get these weeds up?

"What a great idea, I could swoop down while strimming the borders and avoid the rotating cord in the hope that I can root out the offending item!"

But weeds fill the gaps with greenery! Plus the fact that bigger weeds are easier to pull out, so it is not prudent to leave them for now, surely? Despite this lateral thinking weed pulling is best done last as a finishing touch to the garden so don't ask us at the beginning.

At the end of a productive day or weekend, the indigestion caused by sampling lot's of different pies leads to fracas or two and the longing for work, as a respite. Lulled into the false sense of security that your efforts are appreciated there is the distinct possibility that the last word is yet to be said. The next chapter covers the final word, rarely a man's.

6
The Last Word

Who gets the last word? I will let you answer that one.

As far as this short analysis of what women really mean goes there are a few more observations to make on the comments they make and the answers that we would love to say, but decide not to because it will make things worse.

As time goes by couples grow older together and agree to disagree on day-to-day issues. Some couples overdo the 'nag pie' and one or the other throw the towel in and off they go seeking the green grass in the next field, unfortunately the green grass is normally concrete and their jump over the fence results in a bit more pain when they land with a thud. As they meander through life they might be lucky and find a new soul mate and the whole cycle starts over again, from honeymoon period to full-blown buffet tables packed with pies.

Partners are not the only choux chef's, mothers also hold up the family traditions of baking, and this time its nothing to do with baking a coffee cake or a lemon cake for the coffee morning or for the church fundraiser. Maybe it is a generation thing, for the sons in their 30's, 40's and 50's, mother might be a war child when rationing ruled their lives and value for money was their education. Buy it when you can afford to and a credit card is evil. Oh how you do worry her with your disregard for being sensible in everything that you do.

On the other hand it might be a paternal thing, a need to keep the offspring in line with traditional thinking and even after 20 plus years out of the family home a slice of 'nag pie' is deserved. Cheeky wee monkey's that we are!

I don't know about you but I say things to my daughter that my parents said to me, what the heck is that all about? Worse still is hearing a grandmother say the chilling things that we used to hear decades before, this time bypassed as it goes straight to the next generation.

Oh blimey I will be in trouble when mother reads this but in tribute to the slice of 'nag pie' served up by mothers across the globe, here are a few little gems that you might relate to.

Been too busy to come and see your old mother?

Ahh, the classic guilt trip question or comment. Forget the fact that you are holding a job down, in a relationship which requires work, raising children and or trying to keep hold of a little time for your own pursuits; not having the decency to make a regular visit clearly shows what a crap son you are!

If you miss a week the phone will ring and without hesitation the guilt phrase comes into the brief conversation. If you are getting 'nag pie' at home already then this is the icing on the cake, or pie. Brilliant now you are in the doghouse offsite too.

Edna passed away, after a long illness.... send Alf a card

Edna who? Never heard of her, wait a minute you mean that grumpy old lady that always asked how my older brother was and never had a thought to how I was, ever.

Being instructed to send a card to Alf, no known address, to convey sympathy that he has lost his wife, is not a request it is mandatory. If you are a card person then you probably have a few spares in the card box, no wait that's old people that keep a card box isn't it, my mistake. If like most normal people you don't keep a collection of blank cards for every occasion then this means a trip to the card shop, write a few lines of insincere drivel to someone that you don't know or can't remember from forty years ago when you were dragged to church every Sunday. Alf, bless him, who is in grief will probably confuse you with your brother anyway when he reads the card. Makes sense to me, not!

You don't care whether I'm alive or dead do you?
"Of course I do, no really I do...honestly I do, ok you got me"

Faced with a choice of your mother moaning about who's riddled with cancer or who needs a hip replacement and a one-way ticket to Switzerland, it is a tough one, 50:50 at best.

Outrageous, I know but what sort of comment is this? Another guilt trip to endure and leaving you with the only option, to suck up and pander, "oh mum of course not, I enjoy our little chats!"

By the way I have already told my offspring that if I turn into a cantankerous old git that she has my permission to leave me to it, and let me fester in my own self-pity. By then I will have learned so much in life that I will be baking my own pies no doubt.

I left a message, why didn't you call me back?

Yes you did, but there wasn't a question just a message that contained, "it's your mother, your not there so don't bother," which in my book means me not being there has scuppered a request for a lift or a light bulb that needs changing and darkness has descended on the apartment, still managed to find the phone though didn't you!

A good son would jump in his car, race round and make sure his mother hasn't fallen over. Pausing at the door impatiently, filled with concern when she doesn't answer the door after three rings. The concern compounded by the fact that he can hear the television and every word spoken by the 'Songs of Praise' presenter introducing a collection of hymns from a small church in Gretna Green, through the letterbox. After getting his keys from the car, the emergency set, he then runs the risk of a charge of manslaughter when he bursts in and gives her a near heart attack. Then the vacant look, a look of puzzlement, "what are you doing here?" Crisis averted only to find that the original call was for a pint of milk and good old Dotty dropped one in earlier.

These false alarms tend to inevitably generate emergency response to specific questions or requests for an urgent call back. That's not the end of it though if between playing the message back and returning the handset to the cradle the phone rings again. Mum again and it stands a chance that the opening gambit will be "you haven't called me back." The gap between playing the message and the chase call might be slightly longer, so prepare an excuse like the need for proper food, not 'nag pie' hence the lack of immediate response. Actually thinking about it just make the call.

How can you afford it?
A holiday to Disney, a new car or a meal with your daughter, all require justification that you are

solvent and woe betide you if you have taken a loan or used a credit card, yes mothers and headmasters use the phrase, genius.

If the card is the payment option then by the end of the third degree you will feel like calling the insolvency practitioner and filing for bankruptcy. The alternative is to tell her you won a competition sponsored by a breakfast cereal brand or that you used your loyalty points earned from other multiple purchases on your card.

Enough of a debacle of mothers, exaggerated or were they?

What about the last word or words, comments that leave you with anticipation for what will follow. Comments that signal the last piece of one pie and the start of a new helping later in the day or tomorrow, can't wait!

Wait until I get you home!
Despite your hope that this might refer to bumping uglies it stands a chance that it won't be fun when you return to the privacy of your abode.

At least the respite will give you the opportunity to rethink the defence strategy and reiterate the plea of innocence with a different angle on the answers.

You've had it now!
No need to worry then the worst is over if the inference that I have already had it, past tense, thankfully it wasn't "your going to get it" because that would imply that IT is still to come and whatever IT is IT doesn't sound pleasant at all.

Seriously it might be the last word but it's tantamount to a threat, do I need police protection? Is "step away from the knives" something I need to rehearse?

Forget it, I'm off to bed

Great now we will both toss and turn all night, one eye open probably, in case the alarm clock magically appears on my head when the wind blows it off the bedside cabinet!

A good piece of advice I once received from a wise old owl was to 'never go to bed on an argument' and what good advice it is. It's only a shame that in attempting to resolve a difference of opinion it normally only leads to a late night and the same outcome, a continuation the following morning. Back we go to the single words where we started in Chapter One, morning, fine and silence; another day another pie!

Although we all hope to learn from mistakes and life experiences when it comes to a new relationship the lessons we remember disappear from memory far too quickly and off we go on a journey of new discovery; the journey is a bit weird though when we recognise a landmark or two, déjà vu it might be with a hint of a groundhog day thrown in for good measure.

Wouldn't it be great to start afresh and never take a bite of another pie, ever! Of course it would but it's how we men and women are wired, nothing will change except the hope that a realisation that some things are not worth it and the best thing we could do in a relationship would be to accept the fact that men say something and women say it another way. The fiddly little things are not important and although lies and deception deserve every crumb of 'nag pie', miscommunication of the innocent shouldn't be treated as guilty of a fictional crime. Live and let live, and bite your tongue people!

Finally, as with all my books, to the forgotten language of Latin, and to the times when men were rarely questioned.

quis vir sono, mulier sumo non sano
(What man utters, woman chooses not to hear)

Thanks for reading this book, if you would like to get in touch or simply keep up to date with information on books and news you are very welcome to contact me via ...

Twitter Follow @ChrisGAuthor

Facebook - Chris Gibson Author Page

Other available books are listed overleaf

Suggested further reading

"Life of Pie – Nag Pie
(Fifty More Shades of Nagging)
by Chris Gibson

The follow up satirical offering to the hit eBook and paperback 'Fifty Shades of Nagging' that this time discusses the development of a woman in the art of nagging in a journey through life, a "Life of Pie Nag Pie". Counter argument and analysis of the obvious failings of men is included throughout the book in their own "Life of Bragging" (print length 155 pages)

Published by alliebooks.co.uk available as an eBook by Original eBooks and Original Writing (UK) Limited available from Amazon, iTunes and all good sites
Bulk order paperback copies are available from the publisher and via Createspace, global distributor.
Parent ISBN 978-1-909429-06-2
ePub version 978-1-909429-07-9
Mobi version 978-1-909429-08-6

"Golf Speak Exposed - The Crazy Things That Golfer's Say!
by Chris Gibson

The third funny book penned by Chris Gibson that looks at what millions of golfer's say on courses all over the world to excuse poor shots and offer an explanation or commentary to playing partners. A collection of cliches and over used phrases with some alternative answers that could be said in reply, save the need for etiquette that the great game dictates! (print length 88 pages)

Published by alliebooks.co.uk available as an eBook by Original eBooks and Original Writing (UK) Limited available from Amazon, iTunes and all good sites
Bulk order paperback copies are available from the publisher and via Createspace, global distributor.
Parent ISBN 978-1-909429-09-3
ePub version 978-1-909429-10-9
Mobi version 978-1-909429-11-6

(Business books by the author)

**"Franchising Exposed – A Definitive Guide
for anyone looking to buy a franchise or develop
a franchise concept"
by Chris Gibson**

Chris Gibson's first book first published in 2011 and
written to help people looking to start a new business
or convert an existing business into a licensed
franchise partnership. Advice and anecdotes that can
help make the right informed decision
(print length 254 pages - demi size 9.2" x 6.1")

*Published by alliebooks.co.uk available as an eBook by Original eBooks and Original
Writing (UK) Limited available from Amazon, iTunes and all good sites
Bulk order paperback copies are available from the publisher and via Createspace,
global distributor.*
Parent ISBN 978-0-9567618-0-4 (paperback 2011)
ePub version 978-0-9567618-8-0
Mobi version 978-0-9567618-9-7

**"Selling, it's not a Mind Trick"
by Chris Gibson & Alan Guinn**

First published in 2012 and written with co-author
Alan Guinn, a veteran of training people all over the
world via selling seminars. Collectively this book is
a combination of over 70 years experience in sales
and selling with tip and advice that are designed to
help sales executives and the CEO alike.
(print length 112 pages)

*Published by alliebooks.co.uk available as an eBook by Original eBooks and Original
Writing (UK) Limited available from Amazon, iTunes and all good sites
Bulk order paperback copies are available from the publisher and via Createspace,
global distributor.*
Parent ISBN 978-0-9567618-5-9
ePub version 978-0-9567618-6-6
Mobi version 978-0-9567618-7-3

"Selling Skills Exposed – Brilliant Sales Techniques"
by Chris Gibson
& Alan Guinn

A revised look at 'Selling, it's not a Mind Trick' published in 2013, with a new 'search friendly' title and to coincide with global availability on Amazon.
(print length 112 pages)

Published by alliebooks.co.uk available as an eBook by Original eBooks and Original Writing (UK) Limited available from Amazon, iTunes and all good sites
Bulk order paperback copies are available from the publisher and via Createspace, global distributor.
Parent ISBN 978-1-909429-03-1
ePub version 978-1-909429-04-8
Mobi version 978-1-909429-05-5

"So…You Want to Buy a Franchise"
by Alan Guinn & Chris Gibson

Written for the US market, although it translates to any language this is essential reading for anyone looking to enter the wonderful world of franchising and start a business. Advice on business planning, operation and sales techniques are also included.
(print length 125 pages)

Published by alliebooks.co.uk available as an eBook by Original eBooks and Original Writing (UK) Limited available from Amazon, iTunes and all good sites
Bulk order paperback copies are available from the publisher and via Createspace, global distributor.
Parent ISBN 978-0-9567618-4-8
ePub version 978-0-9567618-3-5
Mobi version 978-0-9567618-2-8

"Psyched for Life – A New Guide to Decision Making"
by Alan Guinn

First published in 2001, a short book written by Alan Guinn to focus the reader on how to make effective decisions and avoid procrastination.
Published by Alan Guinn available from Amazon
ISBN 978-0-9712707-0-1

17528126R00039

Printed in Poland
by Amazon Fulfillment
Poland Sp. z o.o., Wrocław